The Empar

Cookbook

The Sweet and Savoury Hand-held Pie Recipes

BY: Ivy Hope

Copyright/License Page

Table of Contents

Introduction

An empanada is also known as "pastel" in Brazil and as "pate" in Haiti. You can get empanadas everywhere in Central as well as South-America even though it varies in appearance and names. Although they aren't necessarily the seems identical, and the fillings are different, they certainly taste delicious!

Deep-fried, oven-baked, or vegetarian empanadas, even the recipes for sweet empanada are also included. Such assortment! And each one of them is filled with flavours! Take a journey through the delicious world of empanadas and stumble on the deliciousness concealed within the crust.

The instructions are super easy to follow so that anybody can make and relish them! All the recipes in this cookbook are so easy to prepare that anyone can make them in absolutely no time at all.

The empanadas are the most widely consumed hand-held encrusted pies in the world. They are stuffed with a marvelous array of different ingredients offering simple, amazing flavors, and are ideal for snacking, a daily meal, epicurean dessert, or a great party cuisine.

This recipe book offers a compilation of the most delightful recipes and vital tips on preparing the perfect semi-circle pies for any gathering, from spinach cheese empanadas (Argentina), spicy chorizo empanadas (Mexico), and potato empanadas (Spain), and tomato-onion empanadas (Brazil) to pineapple jam empanadas (Costa Rica). With the succulent and scrumptious recipes, The Empanadas Recipe Book is beautiful, hands-on, and the ultimate guide to make, serve, and enjoy everybody's favourite hand-held pie.

All the recipes in this cookbook have been tried out by our specialists, and they just love each and every part one of them. So, what are you doing here? Go to your kitchen and make some fresh empanada!

Tried and Tested. So GOOD!

Spinach Cheese Empanadas

Crispy empanadas with spinach and mozzarella filling!

Servings: 14

Preparation Time: 30 minutes

Cooking Time: 15 minutes

Ingredients

For Filling

- 1/4 pound mozzarella cheese, grated
- 1/4 pound stir fried spinach
- Salt and pepper to taste

For Crust

- A pack puff pastry sheets, defrosted
- 1/2 cup egg wash (egg plus water)

Method

1. **For Filling**, combine all the ingredients in bowl. Mix well and keep aside.

2. With the help of a large cookie cutter or wide tumbler cut circles 14 equal circles from puff pastry sheets.

3. Preheat the oven to 350ºF.

4. Put a teaspoon of prepared filling in the center of each circle. Fold each circle into a semi-circle. Press the edges together with your fingers. Then, with the help of a fork press the edges and seal them.

5. Place the prepared empanadas on a baking sheet lined with parchment paper. Apply egg wash with a silicone pastry brush to empanadas.

6. Bake empanadas for 15-20 minutes or until they turn golden-brown.

7. Serve hot with chimichurri or salsa.

Green Pea Empanadas

Crispy empanadas with peas and cheddar cheese filling!

Servings: 14

Preparation Time: 30 minutes

Cooking Time: 15 minutes

Ingredients

For Filling

- 1/4 pound boiled peas
- 1/4 pound cheddar cheese, shredded
- Salt and pepper to taste

For Crust

- A pack puff pastry sheets, defrosted
- 1/2 cup egg wash (egg plus water)

Method

1. **For Filling**, combine all the ingredients in bowl. Mix well and keep aside.

2. With the help of a large cookie cutter or wide tumbler cut circles 14 equal circles from puff pastry sheets.

3. Preheat the oven to 350°F.

4. Put a teaspoon of prepared filling in the center of each circle. Fold each circle into a semi-circle. Press the edges together with your fingers. Then, with the help of a fork press the edges and seal them.

5. Place the prepared empanadas on a baking sheet lined with parchment paper. Apply egg wash with a silicone pastry brush to empanadas.

6. Bake empanadas for 15-20 minutes or until they turn golden-brown.

7. Serve hot with chimichurri or salsa.

Potato Empanadas

Crispy empanadas with potato filling!

Servings: 14

Preparation Time: 30 minutes

Cooking Time: 15 minutes

Ingredients

For Filling

- 1/2 pound boiled potatoes, peeled and mashed
- 1 teaspoon ground cumin
- Salt and pepper to taste

For Crust

- A pack puff pastry sheets, defrosted
- 1/2 cup egg wash (egg plus water)

Method

1. **For Filling**, combine all the ingredients in bowl. Mix well and keep aside.

2. With the help of a large cookie cutter or wide tumbler cut circles 14 equal circles from puff pastry sheets.

3. Preheat the oven to 350°F.

4. Put a teaspoon of prepared filling in the center of each circle. Fold each circle into a semi-circle. Press the edges together with your fingers. Then, with the help of a fork press the edges and seal them.

5. Place the prepared empanadas on a baking sheet lined with parchment paper. Apply egg wash with a silicone pastry brush to empanadas.

6. Bake empanadas for 15-20 minutes or until they turn golden-brown.

7. Serve hot with chimichurri or salsa.

Pineapple Jam Empanadas

Crispy empanadas with pineapple jam filling!

Servings: 14

Preparation Time: 30 minutes

Cooking Time: 15 minutes

Ingredients

For Filling

- 1/2 pound pineapple jam

For Crust

- A pack puff pastry sheets, defrosted
- 1/2 cup egg wash (egg plus water)

Method

1. With the help of a large cookie cutter or wide tumbler cut circles 14 equal circles from puff pastry sheets.

2. Preheat the oven to 350ºF.

3. Put a teaspoon of filling in the center of each circle. Fold each circle into a semi-circle. Press the edges together with your fingers. Then, with the help of a fork press the edges and seal them.

4. Place the prepared empanadas on a baking sheet lined with parchment paper. Apply egg wash with a silicone pastry brush to empanadas.

5. Bake empanadas for 15-20 minutes or until they turn golden-brown.

6. Serve hot with chimichurri or salsa.

Tomato Onion Empanadas

Crispy empanadas with stir fried tomato and onion filling!

Servings: 14

Preparation Time: 30 minutes

Cooking Time: 15 minutes

Ingredients

For Filling

- 1/4 pound onion, finely chopped
- 1/4 pound tomatoes, finely chopped
- 1 tablespoon olive oil
- Salt and pepper

For Crust

- A pack puff pastry sheets, defrosted
- 1/2 cup egg wash (egg plus water)

Method

1. **For Filling**, heat oil in a pan over medium flame. Add in all the ingredients and cook for few minutes. Then, remove the pan from heat and keep aside.

2. With the help of a large cookie cutter or wide tumbler cut circles 14 equal circles from puff pastry sheets.

3. Preheat the oven to 350°F.

4. Put a teaspoon of prepared filling in the center of each circle. Fold each circle into a semi-circle. Press the edges together with your fingers. Then, with the help of a fork press the edges and seal them.

5. Place the prepared empanadas on a baking sheet lined with parchment paper. Apply egg wash with a silicone pastry brush to empanadas.

6. Bake empanadas for 15-20 minutes or until they turn golden-brown.

7. Serve hot with chimichurri or salsa.

Blueberry Empanadas

Crispy Empanadas with blueberry jam filling!

Servings: 14

Preparation Time: 30 minutes

Cooking Time: 15 minutes

Ingredients

For Filling

- 1/2 pound blueberry jam

For Crust

- A pack puff pastry sheets, defrosted
- 1/2 cup egg wash (egg plus water)

Method

1. With the help of a large cookie cutter or wide tumbler cut circles 14 equal circles from puff pastry sheets.

2. Preheat the oven to 350ºF.

3. Put a teaspoon of filling in the center of each circle. Fold each circle into a semi-circle. Press the edges together with your fingers. Then, with the help of a fork press the edges and seal them.

4. Place the prepared empanadas on a baking sheet lined with parchment paper. Apply egg wash with a silicone pastry brush to empanadas.

5. Bake empanadas for 15-20 minutes or until they turn golden-brown.

6. Serve hot with chimichurri or salsa.

Chorizo Empanadas

Crispy empanadas with chorizo filling!

Servings: 14

Preparation Time: 30 minutes

Cooking Time: 15 minutes

Ingredients

For Filling

- 1/2 pound crumbled chorizo, stir fried
- Salt and pepper

For Crust

- A pack puff pastry sheets, defrosted
- 1/2 cup egg wash (egg plus water)

Method

1. **For Filling**, combine all the ingredients in bowl. Mix well and keep aside.

2. With the help of a large cookie cutter or wide tumbler cut circles 14 equal circles from puff pastry sheets.

3. Preheat the oven to 350ºF.

4. Put a teaspoon of prepared filling in the center of each circle. Fold each circle into a semi-circle. Press the edges together with your fingers. Then, with the help of a fork press the edges and seal them.

5. Place the prepared empanadas on a baking sheet lined with parchment paper. Apply egg wash with a silicone pastry brush to empanadas.

6. Bake empanadas for 15-20 minutes or until they turn golden-brown.

7. Serve hot with chimichurri or salsa.

Roasted Duck Empanadas

Crispy empanadas with roasted duck filling!

Servings: 14

Preparation Time: 30 minutes

Cooking Time: 15 minutes

Ingredients

For Filling

- 1/2 pound boneless roasted duck breast, shredded

For Crust

- A pack puff pastry sheets, defrosted
- 1/2 cup egg wash (egg plus water)

Method

1. With the help of a large cookie cutter or wide tumbler cut circles 14 equal circles from puff pastry sheets.

2. Preheat the oven to 350°F.

3. Put a teaspoon of prepared filling in the center of each circle. Fold each circle into a semi-circle. Press the edges together with your fingers. Then, with the help of a fork press the edges and seal them.

4. Place the prepared empanadas on a baking sheet lined with parchment paper. Apply egg wash with a silicone pastry brush to empanadas.

5. Bake empanadas for 15-20 minutes or until they turn golden-brown.

6. Serve hot with chimichurri or salsa.

Anchovies Empanadas

Crispy empanadas with anchovies filling!

Servings: 14

Preparation Time: 30 minutes

Cooking Time: 15 minutes

Ingredients

For Filling

- 1/2 pound canned anchovies, chopped
- 1 teaspoon paprika
- Salt To taste

For Crust

- A pack puff pastry sheets, defrosted
- 1/2 cup egg wash (egg plus water)

Method

1. **For Filling**, combine all the ingredients in bowl. Mix well and keep aside.

2. With the help of a large cookie cutter or wide tumbler cut circles 14 equal circles from puff pastry sheets.

3. Preheat the oven to 350°F.

4. Put a teaspoon of prepared filling in the center of each circle. Fold each circle into a semi-circle. Press the edges together with your fingers. Then, with the help of a fork press the edges and seal them.

5. Place the prepared empanadas on a baking sheet lined with parchment paper. Apply egg wash with a silicone pastry brush to empanadas.

6. Bake empanadas for 15-20 minutes or until they turn golden-brown.

7. Serve hot with chimichurri or salsa.

Tandoori Chicken Empanadas

Crispy empanadas with tandoori chicken filling!

Servings: 14

Preparation Time: 30 minutes

Cooking Time: 15 minutes

Ingredients

For Filling

- 1/2 pound tandoori chicken, shredded

For Crust

- A pack puff pastry sheets, defrosted
- 1/2 cup egg wash (egg plus water)

Method

1. **For Filling**, combine all the ingredients in bowl. Mix well and keep aside.

2. With the help of a large cookie cutter or wide tumbler cut circles 14 equal circles from puff pastry sheets.

3. Preheat the oven to 350°F.

4. Put a teaspoon of prepared filling in the center of each circle. Fold each circle into a semi-circle. Press the edges together with your fingers. Then, with the help of a fork press the edges and seal them.

5. Place the prepared empanadas on the baking sheet lined with the parchment paper. Then, apply egg wash with a silicone pastry brush to empanadas.

6. Bake empanadas for 15-20 minutes or until they turn golden-brown.

7. Serve hot with chimichurri or salsa.

Zucchini Empanadas

Crispy empanadas with stir fried zucchini filling!

Servings: 14

Preparation Time: 30 minutes

Cooking Time: 15 minutes

Ingredients

For Filling

- 1/2 pound zucchini, finely chopped and stir fried
- 1 teaspoon ground cumin
- Salt and pepper

For Crust

- A pack puff pastry sheets, defrosted
- 1/2 cup egg wash (egg plus water)

Method

1. **For Filling**, combine all the ingredients in bowl. Mix well and keep aside.

2. With the help of a large cookie cutter or wide tumbler cut circles 14 equal circles from puff pastry sheets.

3. Preheat the oven to 350ºF.

4. Put a teaspoon of prepared filling in the center of each circle. Fold each circle into a semi-circle. Press the edges together with your fingers. Then, with the help of a fork press the edges and seal them.

5. Place the prepared empanadas on a baking sheet lined with parchment paper. Then, apply egg wash with a silicone pastry brush to empanadas.

6. Bake empanadas for 15-20 minutes or until they turn golden-brown.

7. Serve hot with chimichurri or salsa.

Cherry Sauce Empanadas

Crispy empanadas with cherry filling!

Servings: 14

Preparation Time: 30 minutes

Cooking Time: 15 minutes

Ingredients

For Filling

- 1/2 pound ricotta cherry jam

For Crust

- A pack puff pastry sheets, defrosted
- 1/2 cup egg wash (egg plus water)

Method

1. With the help of a large cookie cutter or wide tumbler cut circles 14 equal circles from puff pastry sheets.

2. Preheat the oven to 350°F.

3. Put a teaspoon of filling in the center of each circle. Fold each circle into a semi-circle. Press the edges together with your fingers. Then, with the help of a fork press the edges and seal them.

4. Place the prepared empanadas on a baking sheet lined with parchment paper. Apply egg wash with a silicone pastry brush to empanadas.

5. Bake empanadas for 15-20 minutes or until they turn golden-brown.

6. Serve hot with chimichurri or salsa.

Pumpkin Empanadas

Crispy empanadas with pumpkin filling!

Servings: 14

Preparation Time: 30 minutes

Cooking Time: 15 minutes

Ingredients

For Filling

- 1/2 pound finely chopped pumpkin, stir fried
- 1 teaspoon pumpkin spice
- 1/4 cup castor sugar

For Crust

- A pack puff pastry sheets, defrosted
- 1/2 cup egg wash (egg plus water)

Method

1. **For Filling**, combine all the ingredients in bowl. Mix well and keep aside.

2. With the help of a large cookie cutter or wide tumbler cut circles 14 equal circles from puff pastry sheets.

3. Preheat the oven to 350°F.

4. Put a teaspoon of prepared filling in the center of each circle. Fold each circle into a semi-circle. Press the edges together with your fingers. Then, with the help of a fork press the edges and seal them.

5. Place the prepared empanadas on a baking sheet lined with parchment paper. Apply egg wash with a silicone pastry brush to empanadas.

6. Bake empanadas for 15-20 minutes or until they turn golden-brown.

7. Serve hot with chimichurri or salsa.

Mozzarella Parsley Empanadas

Crispy Empanadas with mozzarella and parsley filling!

Servings: 14

Preparation Time: 30 minutes

Cooking Time: 15 minutes

Ingredients

For Filling

- 1/4 pound mozzarella cheese, shredded
- 1/4 pound stir fried parsley leaves
- Salt and pepper

For Crust

- A pack puff pastry sheets, defrosted
- 1/2 cup egg wash (egg plus water)

Method

1. **For Filling**, combine all the ingredients in bowl. Mix well and keep aside.

2. With the help of a large cookie cutter or wide tumbler cut circles 14 equal circles from puff pastry sheets.

3. Preheat the oven to 350°F.

4. Put a teaspoon of prepared filling in the center of each circle. Fold each circle into a semi-circle. Press the edges together with your fingers. Then, with the help of a fork press the edges and seal them.

5. Place the prepared empanadas on a baking sheet lined with parchment paper. Apply egg wash with a silicone pastry brush to empanadas.

6. Bake empanadas for 15-20 minutes or until they turn golden-brown.

7. Serve hot with chimichurri or salsa.

Fried Banana Empanadas

Crispy empanadas with banana and cinnamon filling!

Servings: 14

Preparation Time: 30 minutes

Cooking Time: 15 minutes

Ingredients

For Filling

- 1/2 pound fried bananas, mashed
- 1 teaspoon ground cinnamon

For Crust

- A pack puff pastry sheets, defrosted
- 1/2 cup egg wash (egg plus water)

Method

1. **For Filling**, combine all the ingredients in bowl. Mix well and keep aside.

2. With the help of a large cookie cutter or wide tumbler cut circles 14 equal circles from puff pastry sheets.

3. Preheat the oven to 350ºF.

4. Put a teaspoon of prepared filling in the center of each circle. Fold each circle into a semi-circle. Press the edges together with your fingers. Then, with the help of a fork press the edges and seal them.

5. Place the prepared empanadas on a baking sheet lined with parchment paper. Apply egg wash with a silicone pastry brush to empanadas.

6. Bake empanadas for 15-20 minutes or until they turn golden-brown.

7. Serve hot with chimichurri or salsa.

Tuna Empanadas

Crispy empanadas with tuna filling!

Servings: 14

Preparation Time: 30 minutes

Cooking Time: 15 minutes

Ingredients

For Filling

- 1/2 pound canned tuna flakes
- Salt and pepper

For Crust

- A pack puff pastry sheets, defrosted
- 1/2 cup egg wash (egg plus water)

Method

1. **For Filling**, combine all the ingredients in bowl. Mix well and keep aside.

2. With the help of a large cookie cutter or wide tumbler cut circles 14 equal circles from puff pastry sheets.

3. Preheat the oven to 350ºF.

4. Put a teaspoon of prepared filling in the center of each circle. Fold each circle into a semi-circle. Press the edges together with your fingers. Then, with the help of a fork press the edges and seal them.

5. Place the prepared empanadas on a baking sheet lined with parchment paper. Apply egg wash with a silicone pastry brush to empanadas.

6. Bake empanadas for 15-20 minutes or until they turn golden-brown.

7. Serve hot with chimichurri or salsa.

Minced Beef Empanadas

Crispy Empanadas with beef filling!

Servings: 14

Preparation Time: 30 minutes

Cooking Time: 15 minutes

Ingredients

For Filling

- 1/2 pound minced beef, stir fried until brown
- 1 teaspoon dry garlic powder
- Salt and pepper

For Crust

- A pack puff pastry sheets, defrosted
- 1/2 cup egg wash (egg plus water)

Method

1. **For Filling**, combine all the ingredients in bowl. Mix well and keep aside.

2. With the help of a large cookie cutter or wide tumbler cut circles 14 equal circles from puff pastry sheets.

3. Preheat the oven to 350ºF.

4. Put a teaspoon of prepared filling in the center of each circle. Fold each circle into a semi-circle. Press the edges together with your fingers. Then, with the help of a fork press the edges and seal them.

5. Place the prepared empanadas on a baking sheet lined with parchment paper. Apply egg wash with a silicone pastry brush to empanadas.

6. Bake empanadas for 15-20 minutes or until they turn golden-brown.

7. Serve hot with chimichurri or salsa.

Jalapeno Empanadas

Crispy empanadas with jalapeño and mozzarella filling!

Servings: 14

Preparation Time: 30 minutes

Cooking Time: 15 minutes

Ingredients

For Filling

- 1/4 pound mozzarella cheese, shredded
- 1/4 pound pickled jalapeño, finely chopped
- Salt and pepper

For Crust

- A pack puff pastry sheets, defrosted
- 1/2 cup egg wash (egg plus water)

Method

1. **For Filling**, combine all the ingredients in bowl. Mix well and keep aside.

2. With the help of a large cookie cutter or wide tumbler cut circles 14 equal circles from puff pastry sheets.

3. Preheat the oven to 350°F.

4. Put a teaspoon of prepared filling in the center of each circle. Fold each circle into a semi-circle. Press the edges together with your fingers. Then, with the help of a fork press the edges and seal them.

5. Place the prepared empanadas on a baking sheet lined with parchment paper. Apply egg wash with a silicone pastry brush to empanadas.

6. Bake empanadas for 15-20 minutes or until they turn golden-brown.

7. Serve hot with chimichurri or salsa.

Raspberry Empanadas

Crispy empanadas with raspberry jam filling!

Servings: 14

Preparation Time: 30 minutes

Cooking Time: 15 minutes

Ingredients

For Filling

- 1/2 pound raspberry jam

For Crust

- A pack puff pastry sheets, defrosted
- 1/2 cup egg wash (egg plus water)

Method

1. With the help of a large cookie cutter or wide tumbler cut circles 14 equal circles from puff pastry sheets.

2. Preheat the oven to 350ºF.

3. Put a teaspoon of filling in the center of each circle. Fold each circle into a semi-circle. Press the edges together with your fingers. Then, with the help of a fork press the edges and seal them.

4. Place the prepared empanadas on a baking sheet lined with parchment paper. Apply egg wash with a silicone pastry brush to empanadas.

5. Bake empanadas for 15-20 minutes or until they turn golden-brown.

6. Serve hot with chimichurri or salsa.

Corn Empanadas

Crispy empanadas with corn and parmesan cheese filling!

Servings: 14

Preparation Time: 30 minutes

Cooking Time: 15 minutes

Ingredients

For Filling

- 1/4 pound parmesan cheese, crumbled
- 1/4 pound corn kernels
- Salt and pepper

For Crust

- A pack puff pastry sheets, defrosted
- 1/2 cup egg wash (egg plus water)

Method

1. **For Filling**, combine all the ingredients in bowl. Mix well and keep aside.

2. With the help of a large cookie cutter or wide tumbler cut circles 14 equal circles from puff pastry sheets.

3. Preheat the oven to 350°F.

4. Put a teaspoon of prepared filling in the center of each circle. Fold each circle into a semi-circle. Press the edges together with your fingers. Then, with the help of a fork press the edges and seal them.

5. Place the prepared empanadas on a baking sheet lined with parchment paper. Apply egg wash with a silicone pastry brush to empanadas.

6. Bake empanadas for 15-20 minutes or until they turn golden-brown.

7. Serve hot with chimichurri or salsa.

Pepperoni Empanadas

Crispy Empanadas with pepperoni filling!

Servings: 14

Preparation Time: 30 minutes

Cooking Time: 15 minutes

Ingredients

For Filling

- 1/2 pound pepperoni, finely chopped
- Salt and pepper

For Crust

- A pack puff pastry sheets, defrosted
- 1/2 cup egg wash (egg plus water)

Method

1. **For Filling**, combine all the ingredients in bowl. Mix well and keep aside.

2. With the help of a large cookie cutter or wide tumbler cut circles 14 equal circles from puff pastry sheets.

3. Preheat the oven to 350°F.

4. Put a teaspoon of prepared filling in the center of each circle. Fold each circle into a semi-circle. Press the edges together with your fingers. Then, with the help of a fork press the edges and seal them.

5. Place the prepared empanadas on a baking sheet lined with parchment paper. Then, apply egg wash with a silicone pastry brush to empanadas.

6. Bake empanadas for 15-20 minutes or until they turn golden-brown.

7. Serve hot with chimichurri or salsa.

Smoked Turkey Empanadas

Crispy Empanadas with smoked turkey filling!

Servings: 14

Preparation Time: 30 minutes

Cooking Time: 15 minutes

Ingredients

For Filling

- 1/2 pound smoked turkey
- Salt and pepper

For Crust

- A pack puff pastry sheets, defrosted
- 1/2 cup egg wash (egg plus water)

Method

1. **For Filling**, combine all the ingredients in bowl. Mix well and keep aside.

2. With the help of a large cookie cutter or wide tumbler cut circles 14 equal circles from puff pastry sheets.

3. Preheat the oven to 350ºF.

4. Put a teaspoon of prepared filling in the center of each circle. Fold each circle into a semi-circle. Press the edges together with your fingers. Then, with the help of a fork press the edges and seal them.

5. Place the prepared empanadas on a baking sheet lined with parchment paper. Apply egg wash with a silicone pastry brush to empanadas.

6. Bake empanadas for 15-20 minutes or until they turn golden-brown.

7. Serve hot with chimichurri or salsa.

Hawaiian Empanadas

Crispy empanadas with pineapple and ham filling!

Servings: 14

Preparation Time: 30 minutes

Cooking Time: 15 minutes

Ingredients

For Filling

- 1/4 pound pineapple, finely chopped
- 1/4 pound ham, finely chopped
- Salt and paprika

For Crust

- A pack puff pastry sheets, defrosted
- 1/2 cup egg wash (egg plus water)

Method

1. **For Filling**, combine all the ingredients in bowl. Mix well and keep aside.

2. With the help of a large cookie cutter or wide tumbler cut circles 14 equal circles from puff pastry sheets.

3. Preheat the oven to 350ºF.

4. Put a teaspoon of prepared filling in the center of each circle. Fold each circle into a semi-circle. Press the edges together with your fingers. Then, with the help of a fork press the edges and seal them.

5. Place the prepared empanadas on a baking sheet lined with parchment paper. Apply egg wash with a silicone pastry brush to empanadas.

6. Bake empanadas for 15-20 minutes or until they turn golden-brown.

7. Serve hot with chimichurri or salsa.

Black Bean Empanadas

Crispy empanadas with mashed black bean filling!

Servings: 14

Preparation Time: 30 minutes

Cooking Time: 15 minutes

Ingredients

For Filling

- 1/2 pound boiled black beans, strained and roughly mashed
- 1 teaspoon ground cumin
- Salt and pepper

For Crust

- A pack puff pastry sheets, defrosted
- 1/2 cup egg wash (egg plus water)

Method

1. **For Filling**, combine all the ingredients in bowl. Mix well and keep aside.

2. With the help of a large cookie cutter or wide tumbler cut circles 14 equal circles from puff pastry sheets.

3. Preheat the oven to 350°F.

4. Put a teaspoon of prepared filling in the center of each circle. Fold each circle into a semi-circle. Press the edges together with your fingers. Then, with the help of a fork press the edges and seal them.

5. Place the prepared empanadas on a baking sheet lined with parchment paper. Apply egg wash with a silicone pastry brush to empanadas.

6. Bake empanadas for 15-20 minutes or until they turn golden-brown.

7. Serve hot with chimichurri or salsa.

Cheddar Coriander Empanadas

Crispy empanadas with cheddar and coriander filling!

Servings: 14

Preparation Time: 30 minutes

Cooking Time: 15 minutes

Ingredients

For Filling

- 1/4 pound cheddar cheese, shredded
- 1/4 pound coriander
- Salt and pepper to taste

For Crust

- A pack puff pastry sheets, defrosted
- 1/2 cup egg wash (egg plus water)

Method

1. **For Filling**, combine all the ingredients in bowl. Mix well and keep aside.

2. With the help of a large cookie cutter or wide tumbler cut circles 14 equal circles from puff pastry sheets.

3. Preheat the oven to 350ºF.

4. Put a teaspoon of prepared filling in the center of each circle. Fold each circle into a semi-circle. Press the edges together with your fingers. Then, with the help of a fork press the edges and seal them.

5. Place the prepared empanadas on a baking sheet lined with parchment paper. Apply egg wash with a silicone pastry brush to empanadas.

6. Bake empanadas for 15-20 minutes or until they turn golden-brown.

7. Serve hot with chimichurri or salsa.

Cream Cheese Chive Empanadas

Crispy empanadas with cream cheese and chive filling!

Servings: 14

Preparation Time: 30 minutes

Cooking Time: 15 minutes

Ingredients

For Filling

- 1/2 pound cream cheese
- 1 tablespoon chives, finely chopped
- Salt and pepper

For Crust

- A pack puff pastry sheets, defrosted
- 1/2 cup egg wash (egg plus water)

Method

1. **For Filling**, combine all the ingredients in bowl. Mix well and keep aside.

2. With the help of a large cookie cutter or wide tumbler cut circles 14 equal circles from puff pastry sheets.

3. Preheat the oven to 350°F.

4. Put a teaspoon of prepared filling in the center of each circle. Fold each circle into a semi-circle. Press the edges together with your fingers. Then, with the help of a fork press the edges and seal them.

5. Place the prepared empanadas on a baking sheet lined with parchment paper. Apply egg wash with a silicone pastry brush to empanadas.

6. Bake empanadas for 15-20 minutes or until they turn golden-brown.

7. Serve hot with chimichurri or salsa.

Apple Cinnamon Empanadas

Crispy Empanadas with apple pie and cinnamon filling!

Servings: 14

Preparation Time: 30 minutes

Cooking Time: 15 minutes

Ingredients

For Filling

- 1/2 pound apple pie filling
- 2 teaspoons ground cinnamon

For Crust

- A pack puff pastry sheets, defrosted
- 1/2 cup egg wash (egg plus water)

Method

1. **For Filling**, combine all the ingredients in bowl. Mix well and keep aside.

2. With the help of a large cookie cutter or wide tumbler cut circles 14 equal circles from puff pastry sheets.

3. Preheat the oven to 350ºF.

4. Put a teaspoon of prepared filling in the center of each circle. Fold each circle into a semi-circle. Press the edges together with your fingers. Then, with the help of a fork press the edges and seal them.

5. Place the prepared empanadas on a baking sheet lined with parchment paper. Apply egg wash with a silicone pastry brush to empanadas.

6. Bake empanadas for 15-20 minutes or until they turn golden-brown.

7. Serve hot with chimichurri or salsa.

Pesto Brie Empanadas

Crispy empanadas with pesto and brie filling!

Servings: 14

Preparation Time: 30 minutes

Cooking Time: 15 minutes

Ingredients

For Filling

- 1/3 pound brie, crumbled
- 4 tablespoons pesto
- Salt and pepper

For Crust

- A pack puff pastry sheets, defrosted
- 1/2 cup egg wash (egg plus water)

Method

1. **For Filling**, combine all the ingredients in bowl. Mix well and keep aside.

2. With the help of a large cookie cutter or wide tumbler cut circles 14 equal circles from puff pastry sheets.

3. Preheat the oven to 350ºF.

4. Put a teaspoon of prepared filling in the center of each circle. Fold each circle into a semi-circle. Press the edges together with your fingers. Then, with the help of a fork press the edges and seal them.

5. Place the prepared empanadas on a baking sheet lined with parchment paper. Apply egg wash with a silicone pastry brush to empanadas.

6. Bake empanadas for 15-20 minutes or until they turn golden-brown.

7. Serve hot with chimichurri or salsa.

Salami Empanadas

Crispy Empanadas with salami and mozzarella filling!

Servings: 14

Preparation Time: 30 minutes

Cooking Time: 15 minutes

Ingredients

For Filling

- 1/4 pound mozzarella cheese, shredded
- 1/4 pound salami, chopped
- Salt and pepper

For Crust

- A pack puff pastry sheets, defrosted
- 1/2 cup egg wash (egg plus water)

Method

1. **For Filling**, combine all the ingredients in bowl. Mix well and keep aside.

2. With the help of a large cookie cutter or wide tumbler cut circles 14 equal circles from puff pastry sheets.

3. Preheat the oven to 350°F.

4. Put a teaspoon of prepared filling in the center of each circle. Fold each circle into a semi-circle. Press the edges together with your fingers. Then, with the help of a fork press the edges and seal them.

5. Place the prepared empanadas on a baking sheet lined with parchment paper. Apply egg wash with a silicone pastry brush to empanadas.

6. Bake empanadas for 15-20 minutes or until they turn golden-brown.

7. Serve hot with chimichurri or salsa.

Blackberry Empanadas

Crispy Empanadas with blackberry jam filling!

Servings: 14

Preparation Time: 30 minutes

Cooking Time: 15 minutes

Ingredients

For Filling

- 1/2 pound blackberry jam

For Crust

- A pack puff pastry sheets, defrosted
- 1/2 cup egg wash (egg plus water)

Method

1. With the help of a large cookie cutter or wide tumbler cut circles 14 equal circles from puff pastry sheets.

2. Preheat the oven to 350°F.

3. Put a teaspoon of prepared filling in the center of each circle. Fold each circle into a semi-circle. Press the edges together with your fingers. Then, with the help of a fork press the edges and seal them.

4. Place the prepared empanadas on a baking sheet lined with parchment paper. Apply egg wash with a silicone pastry brush to empanadas.

5. Bake empanadas for 15-20 minutes or until they turn golden-brown.

6. Serve hot with chimichurri or salsa.

Cherry Tomato Kale Empanadas

Crispy empanadas with tomato and kale filling!

Servings: 14

Preparation Time: 30 minutes

Cooking Time: 15 minutes

Ingredients

For Filling

- 1/2 pound cherry tomatoes, halved
- 1/2 pound chopped kale leaves, stir fried
- Salt and pepper

For Crust

- A pack puff pastry sheets, defrosted
- 1/2 cup egg wash (egg plus water)

Method

1. **For Filling**, combine all the ingredients in bowl. Mix well and keep aside.

2. With the help of a large cookie cutter or wide tumbler cut circles 14 equal circles from puff pastry sheets.

3. Preheat the oven to 350°F.

4. Put a teaspoon of prepared filling in the center of each circle. Fold each circle into a semi-circle. Press the edges together with your fingers. Then, with the help of a fork press the edges and seal them.

5. Place the prepared empanadas on a baking sheet lined with parchment paper. Apply egg wash with a silicone pastry brush to empanadas.

6. Bake empanadas for 15-20 minutes or until they turn golden-brown.

7. Serve hot with chimichurri or salsa.

Cottage Cheese Empanadas

Crispy Empanadas with cottage cheese filling!

Servings: 14

Preparation Time: 30 minutes

Cooking Time: 15 minutes

Ingredients

For Filling

- 1/2 pound cottage cheese, crumbled
- 1 teaspoon ground cumin
- Salt and pepper

For Crust

- A pack puff pastry sheets, defrosted
- 1/2 cup egg wash (egg plus water)

Method

1. **For Filling**, combine all the ingredients in bowl. Mix well and keep aside.

2. With the help of a large cookie cutter or wide tumbler cut circles 14 equal circles from puff pastry sheets.

3. Preheat the oven to 350ºF.

4. Put a teaspoon of prepared filling in the center of each circle. Fold each circle into a semi-circle. Press the edges together with your fingers. Then, with the help of a fork press the edges and seal them.

5. Place the prepared empanadas on a baking sheet lined with parchment paper. Apply egg wash with a silicone pastry brush to empanadas.

6. Bake empanadas for 15-20 minutes or until they turn golden-brown.

7. Serve hot with chimichurri or salsa.

Pear Empanadas

Crispy Empanadas with pear jam filling!

Servings: 14

Preparation Time: 30 minutes

Cooking Time: 15 minutes

Ingredients

For Filling

- 1/2 pound pear jam

For Crust

- A pack puff pastry sheets, defrosted
- 1/2 cup egg wash (egg plus water)

Method

1. With the help of a large cookie cutter or wide tumbler cut circles 14 equal circles from puff pastry sheets.

2. Preheat the oven to 350°F.

3. Put a teaspoon of prepared filling in the center of each circle. Fold each circle into a semi-circle. Press the edges together with your fingers. Then, with the help of a fork press the edges and seal them.

4. Place the prepared empanadas on a baking sheet lined with parchment paper. Apply egg wash with a silicone pastry brush to empanadas.

5. Bake empanadas for 15-20 minutes or until they turn golden-brown.

6. Serve hot with chimichurri or salsa.

Lentil Empanadas

Crispy empanadas with boiled lentil filling!

Servings: 14

Preparation Time: 30 minutes

Cooking Time: 15 minutes

Ingredients

For Filling

- 1/2 pound boiled lentils, strained and roughly mashed
- 1 teaspoon ground cumin
- Salt and pepper

For Crust

- A pack puff pastry sheets, defrosted
- 1/2 cup egg wash (egg plus water)

Method

1. **For Filling**, combine all the ingredients in bowl. Mix well and keep aside.

2. With the help of a large cookie cutter or wide tumbler cut circles 14 equal circles from puff pastry sheets.

3. Preheat the oven to 350°F.

4. Put a teaspoon of prepared filling in the center of each circle. Fold each circle into a semi-circle. Press the edges together with your fingers. Then, with the help of a fork press the edges and seal them.

5. Place the prepared empanadas on a baking sheet lined with parchment paper. Apply egg wash with a silicone pastry brush to empanadas.

6. Bake empanadas for 15-20 minutes or until they turn golden-brown.

7. Serve hot with chimichurri or salsa.

Raisin Cashew Empanadas

Crispy Empanadas with cashew, raisin, and coconut filling!

Servings: 14

Preparation Time: 30 minutes

Cooking Time: 15 minutes

Ingredients

For Filling

- 4 tablespoons cashews, roughly chopped
- 4 tablespoons raisins, roughly chopped
- 3 tablespoons desiccated coconut, unsweetened
- 3 tablespoons raw honey

For Crust

- A pack puff pastry sheets, defrosted
- 1/2 cup egg wash (egg plus water)

Method

1. **For Filling**, combine all the ingredients in bowl. Mix well and keep aside.

2. With the help of a large cookie cutter or wide tumbler cut circles 14 equal circles from puff pastry sheets.

3. Preheat the oven to 350°F.

4. Put a teaspoon of prepared filling in the center of each circle. Fold each circle into a semi-circle. Press the edges together with your fingers. Then, with the help of a fork press the edges and seal them.

5. Place the prepared empanadas on a baking sheet lined with parchment paper. Apply egg wash with a silicone pastry brush to empanadas.

6. Bake empanadas for 15-20 minutes or until they turn golden-brown.

7. Serve hot with chimichurri or salsa.

Roasted Pork Empanadas

Crispy empanadas with roasted pork and gouda filling!

Servings: 14

Preparation Time: 30 minutes

Cooking Time: 15 minutes

Ingredients

For Filling

- 1/4 pound roasted pork, shredded
- 1/4 gouda cheese, grated
- 1 teaspoon ground cumin
- Salt and pepper

For Crust

- A pack puff pastry sheets, defrosted
- 1/2 cup egg wash (egg plus water)

Method

1. **For Filling**, combine all the ingredients in bowl. Mix well and keep aside.

2. With the help of a large cookie cutter or wide tumbler cut circles 14 equal circles from puff pastry sheets.

3. Preheat the oven to 350ºF.

4. Put a teaspoon of prepared filling in the center of each circle. Fold each circle into a semi-circle. Press the edges together with your fingers. Then, with the help of a fork press the edges and seal them.

5. Place the prepared empanadas on a baking sheet lined with parchment paper. Apply egg wash with a silicone pastry brush to empanadas.

6. Bake empanadas for 15-20 minutes or until they turn golden-brown.

7. Serve hot with chimichurri or salsa.

Baked Salmon Empanadas

Crispy empanadas with baked salmon filling!

Servings: 14

Preparation Time: 30 minutes

Cooking Time: 15 minutes

Ingredients

For Filling

- 1/2 pound baked salmon, crumbled
- 1 teaspoon paprika
- Salt and pepper to taste

For Crust

- A pack puff pastry sheets, defrosted
- 1/2 cup egg wash (egg plus water)

Method

1. **For Filling**, combine all the ingredients in bowl. Mix well and keep aside.

2. With the help of a large cookie cutter or wide tumbler cut circles 14 equal circles from puff pastry sheets.

3. Preheat the oven to 350ºF.

4. Put a teaspoon of prepared filling in the center of each circle. Fold each circle into a semi-circle. Press the edges together with your fingers. Then, with the help of a fork press the edges and seal them.

5. Place the prepared empanadas on a baking sheet lined with parchment paper. Apply egg wash with a silicone pastry brush to empanadas.

6. Bake empanadas for 15-20 minutes or until they turn golden-brown.

7. Serve hot with chimichurri or salsa.

French Bean Empanadas

Crispy empanadas with french bean filling!

Servings: 14

Preparation Time: 30 minutes

Cooking Time: 15 minutes

Ingredients

For Filling

- 1/2 pound finely chopped french beans, stir fried
- 1 teaspoon ground oregano
- Salt and pepper

For Crust

- A pack puff pastry sheets, defrosted
- 1/2 cup egg wash (egg plus water)

Method

1. **For Filling**, combine all the ingredients in bowl. Mix well and keep aside.

2. With the help of a large cookie cutter or wide tumbler cut circles 14 equal circles from puff pastry sheets.

3. Preheat the oven to 350°F.

4. Put a teaspoon of prepared filling in the center of each circle. Fold each circle into a semi-circle. Press the edges together with your fingers. Then, with the help of a fork press the edges and seal them.

5. Place the prepared empanadas on a baking sheet lined with parchment paper. Apply egg wash with a silicone pastry brush to empanadas.

6. Bake empanadas for 15-20 minutes or until they turn golden-brown.

7. Serve hot with chimichurri or salsa.

Bell Pepper Empanadas

Crispy empanadas with bell pepper and cheese filling!

Servings: 14

Preparation Time: 30 minutes

Cooking Time: 15 minutes

Ingredients

For Filling

- 1 medium green bell pepper, finely chopped
- 1 medium red bell pepper, finely chopped
- 1/4 pound mozzarella cheese
- Salt and pepper to taste

For Crust

- A pack puff pastry sheets, defrosted
- 1/2 cup egg wash (egg plus water)

Method

1. **For Filling**, combine all the ingredients in bowl. Mix well and keep aside.

2. With the help of a large cookie cutter or wide tumbler cut circles 14 equal circles from puff pastry sheets.

3. Preheat the oven to 350ºF.

4. Put a teaspoon of prepared filling in the center of each circle. Fold each circle into a semi-circle. Press the edges together with your fingers. Then, with the help of a fork press the edges and seal them.

5. Place the prepared empanadas on a baking sheet lined with parchment paper. Apply egg wash with a silicone pastry brush to empanadas.

6. Bake empanadas for 15-20 minutes or until they turn golden-brown.

7. Serve hot with chimichurri or salsa.

Sausage Empanadas

Crispy empanadas with sausage filling!

Servings: 14

Preparation Time: 30 minutes

Cooking Time: 15 minutes

Ingredients

For Filling

- 1/2 pound sausage, finely chopped
- 1 teaspoon paprika
- Salt and pepper

For Crust

- A pack puff pastry sheets, defrosted
- 1/2 cup egg wash (egg plus water)

Method

1. **For Filling**, combine all the ingredients in bowl. Mix well and keep aside.

2. With the help of a large cookie cutter or wide tumbler cut circles 14 equal circles from puff pastry sheets.

3. Preheat the oven to 350°F.

4. Put a teaspoon of prepared filling in the center of each circle. Fold each circle into a semi-circle. Press the edges together with your fingers. Then, with the help of a fork press the edges and seal them.

5. Place the prepared empanadas on a baking sheet lined with parchment paper. Then, apply egg wash with a silicone pastry brush to empanadas.

6. Bake empanadas for 15-20 minutes or until they turn golden-brown.

7. Serve hot with chimichurri or salsa.

Pizza Empanadas

Crispy Empanadas with mozzarella and pizza sauce filling!

Servings: 14

Preparation Time: 30 minutes

Cooking Time: 15 minutes

Ingredients

For Filling

- 1/3 pound mozzarella cheese, shredded
- 4 tablespoons pizza sauce
- Salt and pepper

For Crust

- A pack puff pastry sheets, defrosted
- 1/2 cup egg wash (egg plus water)

Method

1. **For Filling**, combine all the ingredients in bowl. Mix well and keep aside.

2. With the help of a large cookie cutter or wide tumbler cut circles 14 equal circles from puff pastry sheets.

3. Preheat the oven to 350°F.

4. Put a teaspoon of prepared filling in the center of each circle. Fold each circle into a semi-circle. Press the edges together with your fingers. Then, with the help of a fork press the edges and seal them.

5. Place the prepared empanadas on a baking sheet lined with parchment paper. Apply egg wash with a silicone pastry brush to empanadas.

6. Bake empanadas for 15-20 minutes or until they turn golden-brown.

7. Serve hot with chimichurri or salsa.

Goat Meat Empanadas

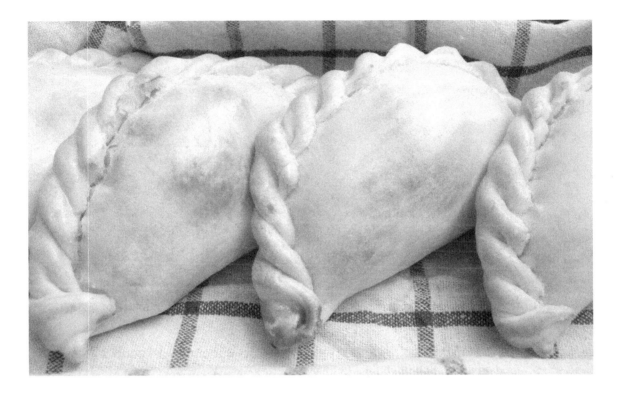

Crispy empanadas with minced goat filling!

Servings: 14

Preparation Time: 30 minutes

Cooking Time: 15 minutes

Ingredients

For Filling

- 1/2 pound minced goat meat, stir fried until brown
- Salt and pepper

For Crust

- A pack puff pastry sheets, defrosted
- 1/2 cup egg wash (egg plus water)

Method

1. **For Filling**, combine all the ingredients in bowl. Mix well and keep aside.

2. With the help of a large cookie cutter or wide tumbler cut circles 14 equal circles from puff pastry sheets.

3. Preheat the oven to 350ºF.

4. Put a teaspoon of prepared filling in the center of each circle. Fold each circle into a semi-circle. Press the edges together with your fingers. Then, with the help of a fork press the edges and seal them.

5. Place the prepared empanadas on a baking sheet lined with parchment paper. Apply egg wash with a silicone pastry brush to empanadas.

6. Bake empanadas for 15-20 minutes or until they turn golden-brown.

7. Serve hot with chimichurri or salsa.

Egg Empanadas

Crispy empanadas with scrambled eggs filling!

Servings: 14

Preparation Time: 30 minutes

Cooking Time: 15 minutes

Ingredients

For Filling

- 1/2 pound cooked scrambled eggs

For Crust

- A pack puff pastry sheets, defrosted
- 1/2 cup egg wash (egg plus water)

Method

1. With the help of a large cookie cutter or wide tumbler cut circles 14 equal circles from puff pastry sheets.

2. Preheat the oven to 350°F.

3. Put a teaspoon of filling in the center of each circle. Fold each circle into a semi-circle. Press the edges together with your fingers. Then, with the help of a fork press the edges and seal them.

4. Place the prepared empanadas on a baking sheet lined with parchment paper. Apply egg wash with a silicone pastry brush to empanadas.

5. Bake empanadas for 15-20 minutes or until they turn golden-brown.

6. Serve hot with chimichurri or salsa.

Strawberry Empanadas

Crispy empanadas with strawberry jam filling!

Servings: 14

Preparation Time: 30 minutes

Cooking Time: 15 minutes

Ingredients

For Filling

- 1/2 pound strawberry jam

For Crust

- A pack puff pastry sheets, defrosted
- 1/2 cup egg wash (egg plus water)

Method

1. With the help of a large cookie cutter or wide tumbler cut circles 14 equal circles from puff pastry sheets.

2. Preheat the oven to 350ºF.

3. Put a teaspoon of filling in the center of each circle. Fold each circle into a semi-circle. Press the edges together with your fingers. Then, with the help of a fork press the edges and seal them.

4. Place the prepared empanadas on a baking sheet lined with parchment paper. Apply egg wash with a silicone pastry brush to empanadas.

5. Bake empanadas for 15-20 minutes or until they turn golden-brown.

6. Serve hot with chimichurri or salsa.

Baked Beans Empanadas

Crispy empanadas with baked beans filling!

Servings: 14

Preparation Time: 30 minutes

Cooking Time: 15 minutes

Ingredients

For Filling

- 1/2 pound baked bean, without sauce
- 1 teaspoon ground cumin
- Salt and pepper

For Crust

- A pack puff pastry sheets, defrosted
- 1/2 cup egg wash (egg plus water)

Method

1. **For Filling**, combine all the ingredients in bowl. Mix well and keep aside.

2. With the help of a large cookie cutter or wide tumbler cut circles 14 equal circles from puff pastry sheets.

3. Preheat the oven to 350°F.

4. Put a teaspoon of prepared filling in the center of each circle. Fold each circle into a semi-circle. Press the edges together with your fingers. Then, with the help of a fork press the edges and seal them.

5. Place the prepared empanadas on a baking sheet lined with parchment paper. Apply egg wash with a silicone pastry brush to empanadas.

6. Bake empanadas for 15-20 minutes or until they turn golden-brown.

7. Serve hot with chimichurri or salsa.

Beef Ball Empanadas

Crispy Empanadas with crumbled beef ball filling!

Servings: 14

Preparation Time: 30 minutes

Cooking Time: 15 minutes

Ingredients

For Filling

- 1/2 pound cooked beef balls, crumbled

For Crust

- A pack puff pastry sheets, defrosted
- 1/2 cup egg wash (egg plus water)

Method

1. With the help of a large cookie cutter or wide tumbler cut circles 14 equal circles from puff pastry sheets.

2. Preheat the oven to 350°F.

3. Put a teaspoon of filling in the center of each circle. Fold each circle into a semi-circle. Press the edges together with your fingers. Then, with the help of a fork press the edges and seal them.

4. Place the prepared empanadas on a baking sheet lined with parchment paper. Apply egg wash with a silicone pastry brush to empanadas.

5. Bake empanadas for 15-20 minutes or until they turn golden-brown.

6. Serve hot with chimichurri or salsa.

Fried Rice Empanadas

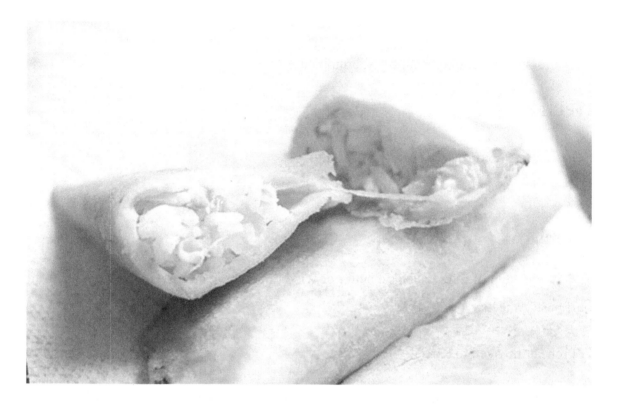

Crispy empanadas with fried rice filling!

Servings: 14

Preparation Time: 30 minutes

Cooking Time: 15 minutes

Ingredients

For Filling

- 1/2 pound cooked fried rice

For Crust

- A pack puff pastry sheets, defrosted
- 1/2 cup egg wash (egg plus water)

Method

1. With the help of a large cookie cutter or wide tumbler cut circles 14 equal circles from puff pastry sheets.

2. Preheat the oven to 350°F.

3. Put a teaspoon of prepared filling in the center of each circle. Fold each circle into a semi-circle. Press the edges together with your fingers. Then, with the help of a fork press the edges and seal them.

4. Place the prepared empanadas on a baking sheet lined with parchment paper. Next, apply egg wash with a silicone pastry brush to empanadas.

5. Bake empanadas for 15-20 minutes or until they turn golden-brown.

6. Serve hot with chimichurri or salsa.

Chilli Chicken Empanadas

Crispy empanadas with chilli chicken filling!

Servings: 14

Preparation Time: 30 minutes

Cooking Time: 15 minutes

Ingredients

For Filling

- 1/2 pound chilli chicken

For Crust

- A pack puff pastry sheets, defrosted
- 1/2 cup egg wash (egg plus water)

Method

1. With the help of a large cookie cutter or wide tumbler cut circles 14 equal circles from puff pastry sheets.

2. Preheat the oven to 350°F.

3. Put a teaspoon of filling in the center of each circle. Fold each circle into a semi-circle. Press the edges together with your fingers. Then, with the help of a fork press the edges and seal them.

4. Place the prepared empanadas on a baking sheet lined with parchment paper. Apply egg wash with a silicone pastry brush to empanadas.

5. Bake empanadas for 15-20 minutes or until they turn golden-brown.

6. Serve hot with chimichurri or salsa.

Ricotta Cheese Empanadas

Crispy empanadas with ricotta filling!

Servings: 14

Preparation Time: 30 minutes

Cooking Time: 15 minutes

Ingredients

For Filling

- 1/2 pound ricotta cheese, crumbled
- 1 teaspoon ground cumin
- 1 teaspoon paprika

For Crust

- A pack puff pastry sheets, defrosted
- 1/2 cup egg wash (egg plus water)

Method

1. **For Filling**, combine all the ingredients in bowl. Mix well and keep aside.

2. With the help of a large cookie cutter or wide tumbler cut circles 14 equal circles from puff pastry sheets.

3. Preheat the oven to 350°F.

4. Put a teaspoon of prepared filling in the center of each circle. Fold each circle into a semi-circle. Press the edges together with your fingers. Then, with the help of a fork press the edges and seal them.

5. Place the prepared empanadas on a baking sheet lined with parchment paper. Apply egg wash with a silicone pastry brush to empanadas.

6. Bake empanadas for 15-20 minutes or until they turn golden-brown.

7. Serve hot with chimichurri or salsa.

Conclusion

The best and superb Empanada recipes from different parts of the world! Come travel with us to the world of easy cooking. The purpose of this recipe book is to epitomize the easy nature of cooking without any special efforts.

In this cookbook, we only focus on Empanadas. This recipe book is actually a complete guide of easy but very innovative recipes. You will learn that even all the recipes are certainly super simple, but they all taste super delicious.

Enjoy!

About the Author

Ivy's mission is to share her recipes with the world. Even though she is not a professional cook she has always had that flair toward cooking. Her hands create magic. She can make even the simplest recipe tastes superb. Everyone who has tried her food has astounding their compliments was what made her think about writing recipes.

She wanted everyone to have a taste of her creations aside from close family and friends. So, deciding to write recipes was her winning decision. She isn't interested in popularity, but how many people have her recipes reached and touched people. Each recipe in her cookbooks is special and has a special meaning in her life. This means that each recipe is created with attention and love. Every ingredient carefully picked, every combination tried and tested.

Her mission started on her birthday about 9 years ago, when her guests couldn't stop prizing the food on the table. The next thing she did was organizing an event where chefs from restaurants were tasting her recipes. This event gave her the courage to start spreading her recipes.

She has written many cookbooks and she is still working on more. There is no end in the art of cooking; all you need is inspiration, love, and dedication.

Author's Afterthoughts

I am thankful for downloading this book and taking the time to read it. I know that you have learned a lot and you had a great time reading it. Writing books is the best way to share the skills I have with your and the best tips too.

I know that there are many books and choosing my book is amazing. I am thankful that you stopped and took time to decide. You made a great decision and I am sure that you enjoyed it.

I will be even happier if you provide honest feedback about my book. Feedbacks helped by growing and they still do. They help me to choose better content and new ideas. So, maybe your feedback can trigger an idea for my next book.

Thank you again

Sincerely

Ivy Hope

Made in the USA
Las Vegas, NV
30 November 2024